Learner autonomy

1: Definitions, issues and problems

David Little

Authentik

Books for language teachers

For Jean

Reprinted 1995

Authentik Language Learning Resources Ltd
is a campus company of Trinity College, Dublin

ISBN 1 871730 02 3

Typeset in Helvetica and Palatino

Foreword

The *Authentik* newspapers and cassettes have helped to promote learner autonomy in a variety of learning contexts, so when Authentik decided to launch a series of short handbooks for language teachers, autonomy was an obvious topic with which to begin. The present volume is concerned with basic definitions, the principal sources of autonomy theory, and the broad implications of the theory for pedagogical practice. Two further volumes on learner autonomy are in preparation: an account of successful classroom practice by Leni Dam and proposals for the development of successful learning strategies by Leslie Dickinson.

The present volume owes its general structure to a lecture I gave at a conference on autonomy in language learning organized by CILT in January 1990. I am grateful to Alan Moys and Lid King for inviting me to give the lecture and thus providing an initial stimulus.

Over a number of years I have benefited greatly from discussions of autonomy, self-direction, learner-counselling, and related issues with Leni Dam, Seán Devitt, Leslie Dickinson, Edith Esch, Philip Riley, and David Singleton. I am particularly grateful to Leni Dam, Seán Devitt and David Singleton for reading and commenting on the first draft of the book.

The book was written in the summer of 1990 during a two-month stay at the University of Hannover. My thanks are due to the authorities of Trinity College, Dublin, for granting me leave of absence; to the Arts and Social Sciences Benefactions Fund, Trinity College, for financial support; and to Claus Gnutzmann for inviting me to be a guest in his department and arranging for me to stay in the Leibnizhaus, a remarkable haven of peace in the middle of a busy city.

Finally, I am grateful to my family for agreeing to do without me for two months; and above all to my wife, not only for her unwavering support in this as in all my other undertakings, but more especially for a tutorial on the role of autonomy in successful child development that began over twenty years ago.

Dublin   David Little
February 1991

Contents

Chapter 1

Preliminaries

Technical terms and the necessity of theory

When we first enter a field of specialist knowledge or experience, we expect to encounter words that are either new to us or else used in an unfamiliar sense. Indeed, our initiation into the field depends crucially on our coming to understand the network of concepts that underlies its specialist vocabulary. But if we remain in the field for any length of time, we are likely to find that the meaning of certain key terms is constantly developing and expanding as the underlying concepts are refined and elaborated. This is true of the most abstruse jargon; it is also true of words in common use that have been appropriated for some special purpose.

The definition and redefinition of terms is a central concern of all theory; for only by a process of constant reflection and clarification can we hope to maintain an adequately coherent overview of any field of activity. Practitioners of all kinds must also be theorists in this sense, if they wish to avoid fossilization. The recent history of language teaching yields two notable examples of the kind of fossilization I have in mind. The terms "communicative" and "authentic" have been buzz words for well over a decade now, and the clusters of issues to which they refer have been the focus of much investigation and discussion. Yet how many language classrooms have been impoverished by an unreflecting assumption that "communicative" language teaching is exclusively concerned with the spoken language, or that "authentic" texts are to be found only in newspapers and magazines? Both terms, of course, have a wider meaning than is often supposed. Because face-to-face oral communication is so central to the human experience of language, it is inevitable and appropriate that it should occupy a corresponding role in language teaching; but in these days of mass media some of the most powerful messages that are communicated within and between societies come to us by means other than the face-to-face encounter. Similarly, newspapers and magazines make up a significant proportion of the reading matter consumed by developed societies - and the success of the *Authentik* newspapers in French, German, Spanish and English testifies to the usefulness of such materials in language learning; but that should not blind us to the fact that recipes and novels, telephone directories and public notices are also authentic texts which language learners may wish or need to be able to cope with.

Learner autonomy has been a central concern among theorists of adult education for well over two decades. More recently it has begun to attract attention in the school sector, and all the signs suggest that "autonomy" is now in the process of attaining the buzz-word status that "communicative" and "authentic" have already enjoyed for many years. It is the purpose of this book to explore what we mean by "autonomy", first by asking what exactly lies behind this deceptively simple word, and then by beginning to tease out how autonomy can be realized in concrete learning situations. In its concern with definitions and their origins the book is theoretical; in its concern with the realities of learning, it seeks to be practical. It is written in the belief that theory is useless if it does not lead to practice, but equally that practice is random and without direction if it cannot be systematically related to a theoretical position.

The concept of learner autonomy has various sources and wide-ranging implications; thus it cannot be satisfactorily defined in a few paragraphs. At the same time, it is necessary to set a framework for the discussion that follows. I shall do this, first by saying what I think autonomy is not, and then by offering a provisional definition.

What autonomy is not

Like any other powerful idea, the concept of learner autonomy arouses strong hostility in some quarters. But more often than not such hostility seems to be based on one or another false assumption about what autonomy is and what it entails. Perhaps the most widespread misconception is that autonomy is synonymous with self-instruction; that it is essentially a matter of deciding to learn without a teacher. Certainly, some learners who follow the path of self-instruction achieve a high degree of autonomy, but many do not. For autonomy is not exclusively or even primarily a matter of how learning is organized.

What might be termed the organizational fallacy emerges again in the assumption that in the classroom context learner autonomy somehow requires the teacher to relinquish all initiative and control. This assumption has two principal sources. The first is a belief that autonomous learners make the teacher redundant, which is closely related to our first misconception. The second source is a belief that any intervention on the part of the teacher may destroy whatever autonomy the learners have managed to attain.

Another misconception that arises in relation to classroom learning is that autonomy is something teachers do to their learners; in other words, that it is a new methodology. This is not entirely false, for learners are unlikely to become autonomous without active encouragement from their teachers. But it is certainly not the case that the development of learner autonomy can be programmed in a series of lesson plans.

A fourth misconception is that autonomy is a single,

easily described behaviour. It is true, of course, that we recognize autonomous learners by their behaviour; but that can take numerous different forms, depending on their age, how far they have progressed with their learning, what they perceive their immediate learning needs to be, and so on. Autonomy, in other words, can manifest itself in very many different ways.

Fifthly, and closely related to our fourth misconception, it is sometimes mistakenly believed that autonomy is a steady state achieved by certain learners. This may well emerge in a teacher's boast that all her learners are autonomous, which seems to set them far apart from ordinary learners. The fact is that autonomy is likely to be hard-won and its permanence cannot be guaranteed; and the learner who displays a high degree of autonomy in one area may be non-autonomous in another.

A provisional definition of autonomy

If learner autonomy is not merely a matter of organization, does not entail an abdication of initiative and control on the part of the teacher, is not a teaching method, is not to be equated with a single easily identified behaviour, and is not a steady state attained by a happy band of privileged learners, then what is it?

Essentially, autonomy is a *capacity* - for detachment, critical reflection, decision-making, and independent action. It presupposes, but also entails, that the learner will develop a particular kind of psychological relation to the process and content of his learning. The capacity for autonomy will be displayed both in the way the learner learns and in the way he or she transfers what has been learned to wider contexts.

In common usage the word "autonomy" denotes a significant measure of independence from the control of others. The concept of learner autonomy similarly implies that the learner enjoys a high degree of freedom. But it is important to insist that the freedoms conferred by autonomy are never absolute, always conditional and constrained. Once this is accepted, many of the misconceptions surrounding autonomy can be cleared away.

Because we are social beings our independence is always balanced by dependence; our essential condition is one of interdependence. Total detachment is a principal determining feature not of autonomy but of autism: autistic children suffer from "severe social impairment, defined as the absence of the ability to engage in reciprocal two-way interaction" (Frith 1989, p.57). The developmental learning that unimpaired small children undergo takes place in interaction with parents, brothers and sisters, grandparents, family friends, neighbours, and so on. Education, whether institutionalized or not, is likewise an interactive, social process. For most of us, important learning experiences are likely to be remembered at least partly in terms of our relationship either with one or more other learners or with a teacher. What is more, our capacity for self-instruction probably develops out of our experience of learning in interaction with others: in order to teach ourselves, we must create an internal substitute for the interaction of home or classroom.

The structure of this book

All the issues touched upon in this introductory chapter are considered at greater length in the five chapters that follow. Chapter 2 is concerned with learner autonomy as a general educational goal. This raises central questions about the psychology of learning and teaching, and they are addressed in Chapter 3. Chapter 4 then considers learner autonomy in terms of what we know about the process of language acquisition. Chapter 5 looks at the possibilities for autonomous learning in adult education and at school. Finally, Chapter 6 addresses some of the practical issues that must be confronted by any autonomous learning scheme.

Chapter 2

Autonomy as an educational goal

Autonomy in adult education

The foundation document for any discussion of autonomy in language learning is the report that Henri Holec prepared for the Council of Europe in 1979 under the title *Autonomy in Foreign Language Learning* (cited here as Holec 1981). Holec's report arose from a general movement in adult education closely associated with the Council of Europe's interest in the concept of permanent education. As Holec notes in his introduction, innovatory proposals of many different kinds belong to this movement by virtue of the attention they pay to

> the need to develop the individual's freedom by
> developing those abilities which will enable him
> to act more responsibly in running the affairs of
> the society in which he lives.   (Holec 1981, p.1)

Holec underlines the inescapably political tendency of this agenda by quoting with approval Janne's (1977) view, expressed in another report commissioned by the Council of Europe, that adult education

> becomes an instrument for arousing an increasing
> sense of awareness and liberation in man, and, in
> some cases, an instrument for changing the envi-
> ronment itself. From the idea of man "product of
> his society", one moves to the idea of man
> "producer of his society". (cit. Holec 1981, p.1)

Clearly, the autonomy that Holec wants to promote is not confined to learning in a more or less formal educational context, but carries over into every other area of life. Indeed, it is explicitly pursued as a means of breaking down the barriers that so often exist between learning and living.

Holec defines autonomy as "the ability to take charge of one's learning" (1981, p.3), which means

> [...] to have, and to hold, the responsibility for all the decisions concerning all aspects of this learning, i.e.:
> - determining the objectives;
> - defining the contents and progressions;
> - selecting methods and techniques to be used;
> - monitoring the procedure of acquisition properly speaking (rhythm, time, place, etc.);
> - evaluating what has been acquired. (*ibid.*)

Traditionally, of course, the teacher is in charge of learning, usually on behalf of some higher agency - school, educational authority, examining board, government department; so that the curriculum is not only imposed on the learner from outside, but has been drawn up without specific regard to his individual experience, needs, interests, and aspirations. The transfer of responsibility for learning from the teacher to the learner has far-reaching implications, not simply for the way in which education is organized but for power relationships that are central to our social structure. For now the learner generates his own purposes for learning; in pursuit of those purposes he determines not only the content of learning but the way in which learning will take place; and he is responsible for deciding how successful learning is, both as process and as goal-attainment. In other words, the curriculum now comes from within the learner, as a product of his past experience and present and future needs; learning is (to borrow a central concept from Ivan Illich's writings) de-institutionalized. Holec does not, of course, imagine that the capacity for autonomous learning is inborn. On the contrary, at several points in his report he insists that it must be developed with expert help. Inevitably, the need for such help becomes a central factor in redefining the role of the teacher in adult education.

Autonomy and schooling

The benefits that should accrue from the development of learner autonomy in adult education may be summarized as follows:

- because the learner sets the agenda, learning should be more focussed and more purposeful, and thus more effective both immediately and in the longer term;

- because responsibility for the learning process lies with the learner, the barriers between learning and living that are often found in traditional teacher-led educational structures should not arise;

- if there are no barriers between learning and living, learners should have little difficulty in transferring their capacity for autonomous behaviour to all other areas of their lives, and this should make them more useful members of society and more effective participants in the democratic process.

Now, formal education at all levels usually claims that it promotes the kind of learning that will enhance the life of the individual and thus enrich society. Inevitably, the question arises whether the arguments for promoting learner autonomy in adult education do not apply with equal force to schooling. After all, it is hardly sensible to leave the formation of responsible and participating citizens to a part of the educational system that is not compulsory and thus touches only a minority of the population, even in the best-endowed western European countries.

As we have seen, one of the chief reasons for promoting learner autonomy in adult education is the desire to remove the barriers between learning and living. Those

same barriers are a central concern of Ivan Illich's book
Deschooling Society (1971, cited here as Illich 1979), one of
the most powerful attacks mounted in recent years against
traditional educational structures. Illich argues that school
institutionalizes values, and thus teaches students to confuse
process and substance:

> The pupil [...] is "schooled" to confuse teaching
> with learning, grade advancement with education,
> a diploma with competence, and fluency with the
> ability to say something new.   (1979, p.9)

In Illich's view school "removes things from everyday use
by labelling them education tools" (1979, p.83).   This
means that even as it offers learners new information and
new experience, school erects a barrier between them and
the intended content and process of their learning. For
Illich schooling is based on the illusion that most learning
is the result of teaching. On the contrary, he insists:

> Most learning happens casually, and even most
> intentional learning is not the result of pro-
> grammed instruction. Normal children learn their
> first language casually, although faster if their
> parents pay attention to them. Most people who
> learn a second language well do so as a result of
> odd circumstances and not of sequential teaching.
> They go to live with their grandparents, they
> travel, or they fall in love with a foreigner. Flu-
> ency in reading is also more often than not a
> result of such extra-curricular activities. Most
> people who read widely, and with pleasure,
> merely believe that they learned to do so in
> school; when challenged, they easily discard this
> illusion.   (1979, p.20)

The examples of successful learning that Illich cites here
are also examples of autonomous learning. In each case

learning is self-motivated, and undertaken in order to fulfil a personal need. It is unlikely, however, that the learners are particularly aware either that they are fulfilling a need or that they are behaving autonomously. This unconscious autonomy is one of the chief hallmarks of effective learning that takes place independently of formal educational contexts.

Whatever one may think of the practicality of the solutions Illich proposes - and they require the dismantling of many structures central to traditional educational systems -, it is difficult to deny that he makes out a powerful case, and not only in relation to the deprived societies of the third world. In our own privileged western European societies, to what extent do elements in the curriculum impinge on the lives that pupils lead - in their heads and in interaction with others - outside school? No doubt functional literacy and numeracy have a direct application to "real life"; and perhaps the more practically oriented subjects like home economics and computer science do too - indeed, this may be a reason for their comparative popularity. But what about history and geography, physics and chemistry? And what, above all, about literature? It is a fair bet that since the beginning of mass formal education, literature for most people has not been something that they have appropriated to themselves, but has been part of the institution of education.

There is, of course, nothing new in this diagnosis. The many curricular and methodological reforms that have been inspired by the concept of learner-centredness are based on a similar analysis. And yet very large numbers of learners - perhaps a majority - remain alienated from the content and process of their learning. The problem is likely to be particularly acute in subjects, including foreign languages, that are usually thought of as belonging to the more "academic" side of the curriculum. This book will argue that the solution lies in learner autonomy of the kind Holec proposes for adult education, but attuned to the different needs of children and adolescents. As I hope to show, learner autonomy is the logical outcome of any attempt to make curricula and classrooms genuinely learner-centred.

From the politics to the psychology of autonomy

Both Holec and Illich present education as an inescapably political process. Positively, it should be the means of giving citizens the freedom to participate fully in the society of which they are members; negatively, the barriers that traditional educational structures can so easily throw up between learning and living are potentially tools of oppression and manipulation.

The fact is, however, that those barriers appear to be erected in the first instance not by political but by psychological factors. They seem to arise, that is, from a mismatch between traditional educational procedures and the ways in which we naturally communicate with and learn from one another. This phenomenon is very thoroughly explored by Douglas Barnes in his book *From Communication to Curriculum* (1976). The distinction that Barnes draws between "school knowledge" and "action knowledge" is essentially the same as the one I have been making between "learning" and "living":

> School knowledge is the knowledge which someone else presents to us. We partly grasp it, enough to answer the teacher's questions, to do exercises, or to answer examination questions, but it remains someone else's knowledge, not ours. If we never use this knowledge we probably forget it. In so far as we use knowledge for our own purposes however we begin to incorporate it into our view of the world, and to use parts of it to

cope with the exigencies of living. Once the
knowledge becomes incorporated into that view of
the world on which our actions are based I would
say that it has become "action knowledge".

(1976, p.81)

This raises the question, what is the relation between
teaching and learning? We have seen that in Illich's view
most learning is not the result of programmed instruction;
and Barnes's book reinforces the view that much of what
goes on in school fails to make an impact on many pupils.
For Barnes, as the above quotation suggests, the problem
is essentially one of communication. We can understand
new information only in terms of what we already know,
and much of the information presented *via* traditional
teaching has little in it that pupils can associate with themselves and their experience. Thus as a communicative
activity, formal teaching - what Bruner (1966) has called
"expository" teaching, the apparently straightforward
transmission of knowledge by teachers to learners - is
highly problematic.

Carl Rogers, the American psychologist and psychotherapist, certainly doubted the feasibility of teaching in
this traditional sense. For him, effective learning could
only arise from the learner's uniquely individual experience; and the only worthwhile learning was learning that
changed the learner's behaviour. Thus in a paper first
published in 1957 he declared:

It seems to me that anything that can be taught to
another is relatively inconsequential and has little
or no significant influence on behaviour.

(Kirschenbaum & Henderson 1990, p.302)

Admittedly he added this note: "That sounds so ridicu-
lous I can't help but question it at the same time that I
present it"; but almost immediately the paper continues:

> I have come to feel that the only learning which
> significantly influences behavior is self-discov-
> ered, self-appropriated learning   (*ibid.*)

and:

> Such self-discovered learning, truth that has been
> personally appropriated and assimilated in expe-
> rience, cannot be directly communicated to an-
> other.   (*ibid.*)

Essentially, Barnes and Rogers are saying the same
thing: learning is possible only to the extent that the
learner is able to integrate the new information that is
being offered with the sum of his experience to date. This
means that any attempt to solve the fundamental communicative problem identified by Barnes must take as its
starting point the learner's perceived needs, his interests,
and his learning purpose.

In the popular imagination, education has to do with
the assimilation of a body of factual knowledge which is
assumed to be static. But of course, knowledge is changing all the time. It is safe to say that the orthodoxy
underlying the teaching of any school subject today is very
different from what it was thirty years ago. In another of
his papers, first published in 1967, Rogers identified the
development of the individual's capacity to cope with
rapid changes in knowledge as the central goal for education:

> Changingness, a reliance on *process* rather than
> upon static knowledge, is the only thing that
> makes any sense as a goal for education in the
> modern world.
>   (Kirschenbaum & Henderson 1990, p.304)

He concluded the same paper with this thought:

> [...] if we are to have citizens who can live construc-

tively in the kaleidoscopically changing world, we
can *only* have them if we are willing for them to
become self-starting, self-initiating learners.
(Kirschenbaum & Henderson 1990, p.321)

This brings us back to the issue of learner autonomy, but
seen less as a political benefit than as a psychological
necessity. If our psychological processes work in the way
that Barnes and Rogers claim (and Holec and Illich strongly
imply), then the case for promoting learner autonomy
begins to look unanswerable. For it appears that effective
and worthwhile learning may actually depend on the
extent to which learners achieve autonomy. This thought
is explored further in Chapter 3, which looks at fundamental issues in the psychology of learning and teaching.

Chapter 3

Autonomy and the psychology of learning and teaching

Learning in child development

Holec's desire to promote autonomy among adult learners; Illich's conviction that most learners in formal educational contexts are alienated from the content and process of their learning; Barnes's distinction between "school knowledge" and "action knowledge"; Rogers's scepticism about the effectiveness of traditional expository teaching - all imply that learning is not a straightforwardly cumulative process, not simply a matter of the learner gradually adding more and more pieces to his stock of knowledge in the way that a child may add blocks of Lego to a developing shape. Rather, learning is to be seen as a process where each increment must be accommodated to what the learner already knows by various processes of adjustment and revision. New knowledge, in other words, necessitates the reorganization of existing knowledge.

This view is very much in line with current accounts of child development, notably those decisively shaped by the work of Jean Piaget and Jerome Bruner. There are important differences between Piaget and Bruner; for example, interaction (and thus language) plays a more central role in Bruner's account of child development than it does in Piaget's. But they share the view that cognitive development is driven by active problem-solving. According to this view, the child is autonomous in the sense that the stimulus to develop comes from within itself and the process of development is not subject to external control. Even in Bruner's model, which allows social interaction a much more central role than Piaget's, the child retains a high degree of independence as it participates in the interdependent processes that provide the material and the context for its problem-solving. It is not proposed, of course, that the child is to a significant extent conscious of the autonomy it enjoys, or that it deliberately manipulates its independence in the interest of more efficient growth; though we should note that a steady increase in self-awareness is an integral part of normal development.

The question then arises, whether there is any qualitative difference between the learning that characterizes normal child development and other kinds of human learning. Certainly, Bruner assumes an essential continuity between developmental and school learning, and the role he assigns to teaching in what he calls the "hypothetical mode" (which involves close co-operation between teacher and learners; see Bruner 1966) is very similar to the role played in child development by verbal interaction of an informal kind. At the same time, all formal education includes some subjects (mathematics and history are examples) that involve modes of thinking not normally encountered outside an educational context. Successful study of such subjects depends crucially on the learner's developing new capacities for abstract thinking - learning, as it were, the syntax of the subject concerned. But in Bruner's view, such specialist capacities are developed by giving children the opportunity to play the role of mathematician, historian, and so on (see Bruner 1977); in other words, by essentially the same processes as are involved in developmental learning.

The psychology of personal constructs

If we are to justify the promotion of learner autonomy in terms of the operation of normal psychological processes, we need a general psychology that is continuous in its essential features with the developmental psychology of Piaget and Bruner. This is provided by the so-called psychology of personal constructs, elaborated by the American psychologist and psychotherapist George Kelly.

Kelly views man as a scientist equipped with a theory, hypotheses, and an insatiable urge to ask questions (*Inquiring Man* is the title of the standard introduction to Kelly's ideas; Bannister & Fransella 1989). By this Kelly meant that each of us has a view of the world; according to that view we have expectations of what will happen in given circumstances; and our lives are a continuous process of hypothesis-testing and theory-revision as we attempt to make sense of the world around us. According to this account, human development is never complete, for it is part of our condition that we must constantly revise our "constructs", the meanings that we attach to events and phenomena, in the light of new experience. The following quotation provides a useful summary of Kelly's position:

> The universe [...] is open to piecemeal interpretation. Different men construe it in different ways. Since it owes no prior allegiance to any one man's construction system, it is always open to reconstruction. Some of the alternative ways of construing are better adapted to man's purposes than others. Thus, man comes to understand his world through an infinite series of successive approximations. [......]
>
> Life is characterized [...] by the capacity of the living thing to represent its environment. Especially is this true of man, who builds construction systems through which to view the real world. (Kelly 1963, p.43)

According to Kelly, a person's "constructions", or "constructs", constitute a system in the sense that they are interrelated; and they are "dichotomous", or "bipolar", in the sense that it is usually easier to think of them as having two poles - *black* versus *white*, *up* versus *down*, *nice* versus *nasty*, *old* versus *new*, and so on (Bannister & Fransella 1989, p.12). Constructs tend to interact with one another hierarchically, as Bannister & Fransella explain (1989, p.13):

> For some people the construct *traditional jazz* versus *modern jazz* may be subsumed as a subordinate implication of the construct *good jazz* versus *bad jazz* and both poles of the construct might be subsumed under the "music" end of the construct *music* versus *noise*. This hierarchical quality of construct systems is what makes the world a manageable place for us. The simple trick of grouping hundreds of different ways of making a living under the construct *jobs* (versus *hobbies* or versus *rest* or versus *vocations*) means that we can then easily handle a whole range of such subordinate constructions. We can offer them to one another, look at their higher, more superordinate implications, add to the category when necessary and so forth.

Where do our personal constructs come from? Clearly, many of them are culturally bound; that is, they derive from the mass of shared assumptions and values which we acquire unconsciously from birth onwards and which help to define the culture, or society, of which we are members. But in their totality, as a system, they are unique to each one of us, for they are constantly shaped and reshaped by our attempts to make sense of the experience that is ours and ours alone.

Personal constructs and learning

How personal construct psychology accounts for learning should already be clear from the necessarily brief and simplified account I have given of Kelly's ideas. Each learner brings his own system of personal constructs to bear on the learning task. In a class comprising learners from several different cultures, there may be very great variation from one construct system to another; whereas in a class whose learners share the same cultural background, the variation may be much less marked. But whatever the composition of the class, individual experience will always ensure that no two learners have exactly the same system of constructs.

According to personal construct psychology, any learning task requires the learner to assimilate new knowledge to his current system of constructs. When the new knowledge is additional information about a subject the learner is already familiar with, learning may proceed without any great difficulty. But when the new knowledge conflicts in some way with the learner's existing system of constructs - perhaps because it explicitly contradicts part of the system, or entails a new way of thinking about something - then learning can be not only difficult but painful.

Although it is usually classified as a version of cognitive psychology, personal construct psychology claims to be all-embracing, accounting for the emotions as well as cognition. For Kelly treats emotions like anxiety, hostility, guilt, threat, fear and aggressiveness as aspects of construct systems that are in process of change (Bannister & Fransella 1989, p.21). The value of this feature of Kelly's psychology is twofold. First, it means that we do not need to go outside the theory in order to explain difficulties in or resistance to learning. Secondly, it amounts to a recognition that learning is often difficult. Like Carl Rogers, Kelly believed that learners and patients in psychotherapy were engaged on essentially the same quest - for a new and fuller understanding that would inevitably challenge their present construct systems and might entail major adjustments. Although it is easy enough to see what Kelly meant, it is important to recognize that by no means all learners - especially learners engaged in formal education - will bring to bear on their learning the same intensity of purpose that the psychotherapy patient may be expected to bring to bear on his healing. For one thing, learners often lack prior interest and personal commitment; for another, genuinely profound learning is not a widespread phenomenon. Although the aim must always be to encourage learners to commit themselves fully to their learning, it is a great strength of Kelly's psychology that it highlights rather than conceals the difficulty of the enterprise.

I have argued that the developing child is autonomous in the sense that its development is not subject to the control of external forces. This autonomy is for the most part unconscious. In Kelly's approach to psychotherapy and teaching, the basic technique is to make the patient or learner aware of his system of personal constructs. For such awareness enables him to identify areas of potential difficulty or conflict in therapy or learning, and gradually to assume conscious control of the process. In other words, Kelly's central purpose is to help the patient or learner to develop a capacity for *conscious* autonomy.

Kelly devised what he called "repertory grid technique" as a method of uncovering patients' personal construct systems. This technique has been applied to many different areas of activity (see Bannister & Fransella 1989); and Salmon (1988) has shown how a simplified version can be used with classroom learners. Essentially, repertory grid technique prompts an exploratory conversation that permits the negotiation of mutual understanding between therapist and patient, teacher and learners.

It is a fundamental claim of personal construct psychology, then, that learning will be facilitated, emotionally as well as cognitively, if learners can be brought to an understanding of their personal construct systems. Again, it is important to emphasize that there is no assumption that this will always be easy to achieve or that successful learning will inevitably follow. Indeed, it is a common experience that attempts to make learners conscious of the demands of a learning task and the techniques with which they might approach it, lead in the first instance to disorientation and a sense that learning has become less rather than more purposeful and efficient. However, when the process is successful, it brings rich rewards.

Thomas and Harri-Augstein (1990, pp.213f.) identify three stages by which a learner moves from the unconscious performance of a task to fully self-organized learning. The first stage is characterized by "dogged practice and repetition"; some level of competence is achieved, but the learner remains totally content- or task-bound. The second stage is characterized by detachment from the task and reflection on it; but the task remains the total focus of attention. In the third stage the focus of attention shifts to the process of learning itself, and this is what provides "the crucial trigger to total self-organization in learning". Thomas and Harri-Augstein note that most learners find it difficult to attain this third stage on their own. This recalls Holec's argument that learners are unlikely to develop a capacity for autonomy without assistance, and brings us again to the question of the teacher's role.

Teachers have personal constructs too

Personal construct psychology provides us with a powerful argument for adopting a learner-centred approach to curriculum and teaching. But if it is true that no two individuals have exactly identical systems of personal constructs, it follows that we must pay as much attention to teachers' as to learners' individuality. Much of my argument so far tends, explicitly or by implication, towards

the conclusion that the teacher must find ways of accom-
modating her teaching to the personal constructs of her
learners. But whatever method she adopts to do this, she
cannot exclude her own system of personal constructs
from the process. Among other things, this means that
teachers owe it to themselves to be thoroughly familiar
with the assumptions, values and prejudices which determine their classroom behaviour.

Salmon (1988, pp.30 pass.) points out that attempts to
explain why some teachers are good and others bad have
tended to focus either on the skills required for effective
teaching or on the personality of the effective teacher. Both
kinds of explanation say little about the content of teaching, which is assumed to be independent of teaching skills
on the one hand and the teacher's personality on the other.
However, if we approach teaching from the perspectives
of personal construct psychology, content is centrally
important because it is inescapable. Classroom learning
involves an encounter between a number of personal
construct systems, all of them having some things in
common but each at the same time uniquely individual;
and there is a sense in which, whatever her subject, the
teacher cannot help but teach herself (Salmon 1988, p.37).
That is, the curriculum that she presents to her learners is
hers and no one else's. However closely she may follow a
prescribed programme, she can only communicate her
unique interpretation of it. I shall return to the issue of the
teacher as the content of her teaching in Chapter 5, when
I discuss the scope for developing learner autonomy in
classrooms. For the moment it is enough to note the
implication that teacher autonomy is a precondition for
learner autonomy. In the next chapter we shall see how
this point is reinforced by the special demands made by
second and foreign language learning and teaching.

Chapter 4

Autonomy in language acquisition and language use

First language development

There is more than one view of the relation between general cognitive and linguistic development. For Piaget cognitive development proceeds independently of linguistic development, though as its necessary precondition; whereas for Bruner the two are more closely related, interacting at certain stages. At the same time, Piaget and Bruner share the view that the acquisition of syntax is a matter of internalizing relations that the child has already come to understand in the external world, which contrasts with Chomsky's insistence that grammatical structures are innate. But whichever side we choose to take in this argument it is clear that the acquisition of a first language, or mother tongue, is an integral part of the development of every normally endowed child. What is more, the process has three defining features in common with the process of cognitive development as understood by Piaget and Bruner.

First, learning a mother tongue shares with other developmental learning the characteristic that it is not merely additive. Research has shown that children do not learn their mother tongue word by word and structure by structure. Rather, they pass through a series of well-defined stages, starting with single-word utterances whose interpretation is closely bound to the context in which they are produced, and ending with strings of words that deploy the fully-developed structures of the language in question. As the child passes from one stage to the next, its existing linguistic knowledge must be adjusted to accommodate new structural features.

Secondly, there is no separation between learning language and using language. General cognitive development proceeds, not only in order that children should be able to solve the problems they encounter in interaction with their environment, but as a result of their solving them. In the same way, language acquisition proceeds, not only in order that children should be able to communicate with their parents, but as a result of their communicating with them.

Thirdly, children progress from one stage of linguistic development to the next when they are ready, and not when they are told to do so by their parents or some other external agency. In other words, language acquisition, like general cognitive development, proceeds on the initiative of the child as it gradually learns to meet the communicative needs generated by its interaction with the environment. Thus, the largely unconscious autonomy that I have argued is an essential feature of general cognitive development is also an essential feature of first language acquisition.

This autonomy has two aspects. The first has to do with the (unconscious) agenda by which linguistic development proceeds; the second has to do with the social freedom that the child enjoys to interact with parents, siblings, relations, caregivers, and so on. Whatever attempts may be made to impose control at a later stage, in the pre-school years it is usually the child who decides when it will talk and what it will talk about; though the range of possibilities will be constrained by the environment in which it finds itself.

Now, it seems to be the case that all normally endowed children will develop the same basic internal grammar, or unconscious knowledge of the structure of their mother tongue, provided they receive "input" and have opportunities to interact with other people. But differences in social circumstances will obviously lead to differences in the types of interaction available to the developing child; and this in turn will lead to differences in communicative repertoire from one child to another. In terms of the argument in Chapter 3, different experiences will lead to the formation of different sets of personal constructs. These differences are likely to increase when children move beyond the pre-literate stage. For one thing, the development and exercise of literacy skills involves all our cognitive faculties - in other words, fully engages our whole system of personal constructs. For another, reading and writing are not acquired autonomously as part of natural development; they must be taught, or at least learned by conscious effort. And consciousness of a learning task implies the possibility of the learner's having an attitude to it, which in turn admits the possibility of widely differing degrees of success.

Second language acquisition

So-called "naturalistic" second language acquisition - that is, the learning of a second language without benefit of instruction - proceeds in essentially the same way as first language development. Social interaction generates communicative needs and provides the learner with input; and the learner's effort to meet his communicative needs by using the target language gradually produces learning. What is more, although the detailed interpretation of the research evidence is not beyond dispute, it seems fairly clear that second language acquisition, like first language development, is characterized by a succession of stages; that the structures of a language are internalized in a more or less fixed order, irrespective of such individual factors as the learner's mother tongue, social background, or age (for an accessible discussion of the evidence, see Long 1987).

But whereas children acquiring the same mother tongue define themselves as native speakers of the language in question by developing the same internal grammar, "naturalistic" second language acquisition has the greatest possible variety of outcomes, ranging from near-native competence at one end of the spectrum to the most minimal communicative repertoire at the other. Of the many reasons that can be advanced to explain this, perhaps the most obvious are social and attitudinal; and they are directly related to the issue of autonomy.

In Chapter 2 I quoted Illich's argument that most successful learning takes place independently of teaching (see p.9 above). Among the examples he gives are people who learn a foreign language by going to live with their grandparents or by falling in love with a foreigner. In either case the social situation of such learners is likely to be highly favourable. Not only are they in a friendly and supportive environment, among people who have a strong personal interest in their learning success; they are also confronted by a range of communicative possibilities no less great than that of the child acquiring its mother tongue. Their situation confers on them much the same kind of social autonomy as is enjoyed by the child learning its mother tongue, and this (we may hypothesize) allows free rein to the acquisition process.

The case of the migrant worker is very different. At home, with his family or in lodgings with other migrant workers, he speaks his mother tongue, and this is the medium through which he conducts his social life. At work his colleagues are likely to be other migrant workers, perhaps speaking the same language as himself. Thus he needs to understand and speak the language of the host community only in a limited number of situations, most of them involving encounters with figures of authority. He receives a narrow range of input from a narrow range of communicative events. In all probability he will not progress beyond the minimal communicative repertoire that he needs for survival. He may well form a negative image of the host community, and this will further reduce the likelihood of his learning its language. It is difficult to imagine a situation further removed from that of the teenager learning his grandparents' language or the bride learning her husband's language. In the absence of any kind of social autonomy, we cannot expect the migrant worker to develop the psychological autonomy that characterizes first language development and successful second language acquisition.

Implications for language teaching

The principal goal of second and foreign language teaching has always been to enable learners to use the language in question as a medium of communication, defined in the broadest sense. Communicative efficiency in the target language community depends on learners having the independence, self-reliance and self-confidence to fulfil the variety of social, psychological and discourse roles in which they are cast. It depends, that is to say, on their achieving a substantial degree of autonomy as language users. In order to maintain this autonomy, they must be aware of the social requirements of the different situations in which they are called upon to use the target language; sensitive to the varying psychological relations they will have to the different persons with whom they must communicate; and capable equally of taking initiatives and responding to the initiatives of others. This is a tall order, even when the communicative repertoire aimed at is carefully limited and precisely defined on the basis of an analysis of the learners' needs. It is an especially tall order when, as happens in many formal educational contexts, the learners have no prior interest in learning a foreign language.

Some approaches to language teaching have concentrated the classroom effort on mastery of the structures of the target language - by exposition and practice in the grammar-translation tradition, by drilling structures in the audio-lingual and audio-visual methods. Usually such approaches have included opportunities for free expression in the target language, but they have tended to assume that learners will convert their classroom knowledge into communicative competence principally through subsequent contact with the target language community. There are two flaws in this assumption. First, in reality most learners do not come into frequent or sustained contact with the target language community; and secondly, analytical knowledge acquired in the classroom is not necessarily continuous with the internalized knowledge on which linguistic fluency rests.

As we have seen, research into first and "naturalistic" second language acquisition has shown that the human brain has a characteristic way of learning language, gradually analysing an internal grammar out of the input it receives. It would be surprising if language teaching in more or less formal educational contexts could circumvent these highly complex unconscious processes. In fact, research into classroom language learning has uncovered evidence of the same developmental orders as have been observed in "naturalistic" learners. It seems that instruction may have a positive effect only when it either reinforces the features of the target language that the learners are ready to internalize or is focussed on types of communication that allow learners to pay particular attention to the form of their utterance (for a review of the evidence, see Long 1987).

It is the virtue of genuinely communicative approaches to language teaching that they attempt to take account of these matters. Recognizing that "naturalistic" language

tions. It is an important feature of this approach that at the end of each project-phase of four or five weeks the learners must form new groups. This prevents the establishment of cliques, ensures that in the course of a school year each learner works at least once with all the other members of the class, and insists on maintaining the class as a single open society.

In much formal education language is taken for granted. It may be necessary for learners to acquire new stylistic habits appropriate to the "syntax" of the subjects they are studying, but usually these are assumed to be an inevitable by-product of successful learning rather than one of its central concerns. Certainly, the educational approaches we were concerned with in Chapter 2 recognize the importance of language for learning. Barnes, for example, writes: "Through language we both *receive* a meaningful world from others, and at the same time *make meanings* by re-interpreting that world to our own ends" (1976, p.101). But still, language is seen essentially as medium rather than content. In the second or foreign language class, by contrast, the target language has always been content but all too rarely medium. It is central to the argument of this chapter that successful language learning requires language to be simultaneously medium and content.

We have seen how in the second of our two classrooms learners' personal constructs are engaged through ongoing processes of negotiation. This has the effect of interesting them in the language learning task. But successful second or foreign language learning is a matter not only of engaging learners' personal constructs: to some extent those constructs must also be extended and reshaped by and in the target language. In "naturalistic" second language acquisition this happens unconsciously as a result of social interaction. In the classroom we certainly want to exploit natural processes of acquisition by having learners use the target language as the medium of their interaction and learning. But the negotiation that plays a central role in any attempt to promote learner autonomy requires that we make explicit not only learners' attitudes, assumptions, and goals, but some of the central features of the target language. In other words, we need to supplement behavioural with analytical learning, and we need to develop techniques for bringing these two types of learning together. I have already mentioned the possibility of a "brain-storming" exploration of the vocabulary appropriate to a particular topic, which can prepare learners to receive and respond to a text that will provide them with new information: new words, new meaning relations between words, and perhaps new structures. I conclude this chapter with an account of a chain of activities that we have used with learners of French, German and English at many in-service days sponsored by Authentik. It seems to us to suggest the beginnings of a pedagogy that helps to develop learners' autonomy as language acquirers by basing the language learning task directly on an exploration of their personal constructs.

To begin with, learners are given a jumble of perhaps twenty-five or thirty words and phrases that have been derived from an authentic text. Working in groups of three or four, their first task is to sort the words and phrases into four overlapping categories - TIME, PERSON, PLACE, EVENT. This requires them to think about words as individual tokens, but it also encourages them to begin to consider possible semantic and syntactic relations between words. The second task is to use the words to construct a story outline. This continues the process of drawing directly on learners' personal constructs, but since it is a group activity it also demands negotiation and compromise between learners. When the story outline is complete, the learners are given a simplified version of the authentic text containing all the words they were given at the beginning of the activity chain. Their next task is to use this simplified text as a linguistic resource to expand their story outline into a fully developed text. It is up to them to decide whether or not their story should be adjusted to coincide with the simplified text. When they have finished producing their text, they are given the full authentic text to compare it with.

It is our experience that this procedure enables learners to derive a great deal more meaning from the authentic text, and thus potentially to learn a great deal more from it, than they would if they simply tried to read it. For the activities that have led up to the authentic text have gradually helped them to develop their own target language construct as a basis for receiving the authentic text. (Many of the exercises in the *Authentik* newspapers and cassettes are variations on this approach; further examples and a fuller discussion are to be found in Little et. al. 1988 & 1989.)

Chapter 5

Autonomy in two kinds of learning environment

The argument so far

I began Chapter 2 by showing that in adult education the concept of learner autonomy is closely associated with the desire to remove the barriers that often exist between learning and the rest of living; the assumption being that successful learners can carry their capacity for autonomous behaviour into every other area of their lives. I then argued that the same concern to remove barriers between learning and living provides a powerful argument for promoting autonomous learning at school. And I concluded the chapter by suggesting that the source of autonomy theory is psychological, having to do with how we learn, and raised the question whether perhaps effective learning takes place at all only to the extent that we achieve, whether consciously or unconsciously, a sufficient degree of autonomy.

In Chapter 3 I began by noting that for Piaget and Bruner cognitive development proceeds on the basis of the child's problem-solving interaction with its environment, according to an agenda that is internal to the child and not susceptible to external minipulation or control. In this the child may be said to enjoy a large measure of unconscious autonomy. I then argued that the psychology of personal constructs provides us with a general psychology of learning which is founded on essentially the same view of human cognitive operations as the developmental psychology of Piaget and Bruner. It argues that learning will be possible to the extent that our personal constructs enable us to understand and assimilate the new knowledge in question; and that where the new knowledge is in conflict with our constructs learning will be difficult, perhaps even painful, and may be successfully resisted. I concluded the chapter with the thought that not only learners but teachers have personal constructs, and that as a consequence each teacher's interpretation of the curriculum is necessarily unique; so that autonomy is an issue for teachers as well as learners.

I began Chapter 4 by pointing out that first language acquisition is similar in three respects to cognitive development in general. First, it is not merely additive; the absorption of new linguistic knowledge requires constant reorganization of what is already known. Secondly, in first language acquisition there is no separation between language learning and language use; indeed, language use is the indispensable channel of language learning. Thirdly, the child acquiring its mother tongue is autonomous in the sense that it proceeds according to an internal agenda that cannot be changed by external intervention. I then noted that "naturalistic" second language acquisition proceeds *via* the same processes of social interaction as first language development, and that it too is characterized by clearly defined stages. Moreover, research has revealed that second language learners in the classroom pass through the same developmental stages as "naturalistic" second language learners. This was taken to imply that language classrooms must provide learners with plenty of input and ample opportunity for interaction with and through the target language. In particular, learners must be allowed the social autonomy which is necessary to successful "naturalistic" second language acquisition because it guarantees access to a wide variety of discourse roles. I argued that such autonomy is likely to be achieved by processes of negotiation that invite learners to explore and make explicit their personal constructs. Finally, I suggested that in order to help learners to achieve psychological as well as social autonomy in their learning, it is necessary to engage their personal constructs in the linguistic as well as the social dimension of the learning process.

The remainder of this book is concerned with practical issues in the implementation of learner autonomy. In this chapter I consider the possibilities for, but also the apparent limitations on, the implementation of autonomy outside and inside the full-time educational system; while in Chapter 6 I discuss some of the major issues and problems that autonomous learning schemes have to confront.

Autonomous learning outside the full-time educational system

In practical as well as psychological terms it is easy to see why adult education should be learner-centred and should seek to promote autonomous, self-organized learning. For one thing, adults who undertake a course of learning usually do so because they want to fulfil some personal or professional need. Thus they should be able to specify learning targets that are both precise and unique to themselves. Furthermore, because learning is only a small part of their lives, only they can decide when and how they should learn, and only they can decide when the learning process has achieved its purpose. Also, many adults who undertake language learning for professional purposes have needs so distinctive that they cannot be met by commercially available learning materials or general language courses. For example, a German scientist who already has quite fluent "general" English may need to develop skills in argument and debate within his own discipline so that he can participate in international seminars where the working language is English; or a senior member of the clerical staff of an English firm exporting to Italy may need to develop a limited range of skills in written communication to handle correspondence by letter, fax and telex. In such cases the best learning materials are likely to be authentic texts (in print, audio, or video) that exemplify the repertoire the learner is aiming at, together with a set of strategies for exploiting them.

Of course, we should not expect the adult learner to be able to define and meet his learning targets without expert assistance. He will almost certainly need help in specifying what it is he should learn and translating that into a coherent learning programme; in deciding how to make best use of the limited time that he can devote to learning; in finding appropriate materials to work with and devising strategies to exploit them effectively; and in learning how to evaluate his progress. Ideally, our learner needs to join a scheme that is explicitly devoted to the promotion of autonomous language learning. Such a scheme is likely to be founded on a combination of learning resources and learner counselling, the aim of the latter being to help learners achieve an ever-clearer understanding of why they are learning, what they are learning, and how they are learning (for a discussion of some of the fundamental issues, see Riley (ed.) 1985 and Little (ed.) 1989; for a case study, see Little & Grant 1986).

Schemes of this kind are not widespread, however, and most adults who feel a need to learn a foreign language find themselves enrolling for a language course that is organized along much the same lines as school. It is divided into terms; it is probably based on a course book; there may be an examination or test to pass at the end of the year; and the teacher's relation to the class may well be traditional in the extreme. Certainly the promotion of learner autonomy is as desirable in these as in any other circumstances, for the reasons I have advanced in earlier chapters. However, the issues involved are essentially the same as those that must be confronted by anyone wanting to promote autonomous learning at school.

Autonomous learning at school

Learners engaged in full-time education are different in a number of important respects from the adult learners we have just been considering. They are younger; the course of their life has not yet been determined; their interests are likely to be age-related and may thus be short-lived; they are learning because they have to, and not necessarily because they want to; and their learning ends not when they have achieved their learning targets but according to a timetable usually prescribed by their date of birth.

For those inside the system it can easily seem that there are so many constraints, so many factors over which teachers and learners have no control, that learner autonomy is an impossible dream. They may be persuaded by arguments of the kind I have been advancing, and they may long to explore ways of making their classrooms places where learning and living are one and the same thing. But they are convinced that the system is so all-powerful and inflexible that autonomous learning cannot possibly happen for them. No doubt it does happen, in a handful of specially favoured situations, but as a general goal it is simply not practicable; the syllabus and the examinations just do not permit it. This counsel of despair is founded, I believe, on three misconceptions.

The first misconception has to do with the power of the syllabus, which is supposed to determine everything that the teacher does in the classroom. This misses the point I made towards the end of Chapter 3, that precisely because teachers have personal constructs they cannot help but have a unique understanding of the syllabus; so that their teaching cannot be identical to anyone else's. The syllabus has not yet been written that prescribes exactly what the teacher must do in every class from the beginning to the end of her pupils' learning. But even if such a document were devised - effectively a script for every lesson - the teacher's individuality would still ensure that her performance of the script was unlike anyone else's. No doubt teaching must always have an eye on the syllabus; but even the most slavish disciple of the syllabus cannot avoid taking a host of individual decisions and initiatives in order to teach her classes. Why should those decisions and initiatives not work in favour of learner autonomy?

The second misconception underlying our counsel of despair is that the examinations are a barrier to the development of learner autonomy because they predetermine the content of learning. This was more likely to be true at a time when foreign language syllabuses gave a central role to prescribed (usually literary) texts; though even then it was normally not the intention of the syllabus that learners should read only the texts that were prescribed. But nowadays prescribed texts play a much reduced role in examination programmes, which by and large seek to test skills rather than content. Certain skills inevitably constrain content; for example, a test of candidates' ability to understand public notices or public announcements must be based on an appropriate range of possible instances. But other skills - of reading and listening comprehension, of general conversation, of letter-writing - are, relatively speaking, content-free. And it must be so; for there is no way of guaranteeing that all candidates will have been exposed to exactly the same input, leading them to a mastery of exactly the same words and structures (in terms of the argument of Chapter 3, of course, no two learners will ever learn exactly the same things). It has often been said, but it is nonetheless true, that it is does not help learners to be taught with only the examination in mind; for this inevitably limits their learning and gives rise to precisely the disjunction between learning and living that autonomy should help us to avoid.

The third misconception underlying our counsel of despair has to do with the content of learning. Even allowing that neither the syllabus nor the examination can fully specify what is to be learned, many teachers remain convinced that there is a certain amount of ground that must be covered, certain things that must be taught. Usually these "things" are elements of the target language grammar - more often than not, features of morpho-syntax; so that the concern about content is focussed not on input but on the grammatical repertoire that learners should derive from input. This concern originates in traditional beliefs about the appropriate modes of teaching, for it is clearly based on the conviction that it should be possible to teach language, and especially grammar, by expository means. But the fact is, no amount of teaching has ever been able to guarantee learning, in second and foreign languages or any other subject. And to insist on believing that it can is to fly in the face of a growing body of research evidence. As we saw in Chapter 4, second and foreign languages are learned (or internalized) by the same interactive processes as first languages. The explicit treatment of features of the target language system can probably support these processes, but it certainly cannot replace them. The most successful learners are likely to be those who are constantly interacting with and through the target language, receiving and expressing meanings that are important to them.

To the extent that it defines the content of learning in explicit linguistic terms, a course book can easily stand in the way of efficient language acquisition. At one time course books systematically took learners through the grammar of the target language, each unit dealing with a different part of speech or a different structure; nowadays they tend to focus on communicative functions. But in either case, whatever the thematic content of each unit, its underlying aim will be to teach a feature of the target language. This means that the structure and rhythm of lessons are likely to be determined, as Devitt (1989) has shown, not by the way a particular theme unwinds, but by the teacher's sense of how the learners are coping with the linguistic feature that provides the teaching point for the unit.

There are various ways of trying to solve this problem. One is to retain the course book but supplement it with authentic materials, which is how most teachers use the *Authentik* newspapers and cassettes. This has the advantage of retaining the structure that the course book provides, but the disadvantage that it may turn out to be very difficult to break the tyranny of the course book. A second solution is to retain the course book, but make the learners responsible for teaching one another. This approach to the development of learner autonomy has been used with great success by Jean-Pol Martin of the University of Eichstätt in Bavaria. A third solution is to replace the course book with materials that teach parts of other curriculum subjects through the target language; this approach is advocated by Devitt (1989). A fourth solution is to replace the course book with authentic materials provided by the teacher and/or the learners - a minority of teachers now use *Authentik* as their principal teaching/learning resource. These last two solutions have the advantage that the content of learning, in the sense of input, remains unstructured. However, unstructured input materials need to be supplemented with explicit information about the target language, at least in the form of a grammar and a dictionary, in order that behavioural may be supplemented by analytical learning. In each case, of course, the development of learner autonomy depends not on the content materials *per se*, but on the relation that the learners establish to them.

Chapter 6

Issues and problems in the implementation of autonomy

The teacher

By now it should be clear that, so far from requiring him to relinquish control in the classroom, the development of learner autonomy will depend crucially on the initiatives the teacher takes - learners will not develop their capacity for autonomous behaviour simply because he tells them to. The question is, what kinds of initiative should the teacher take, and in what ways are they likely to differ from the initiatives he is used to taking?

I argued in Chapter 3 and again in Chapter 5 that every teacher necessarily has his own unique interpretation of the syllabus he is responsible for teaching. Perhaps the first step he should take towards developing autonomy in his learners is to negotiate a joint interpretation of the syllabus with them. This will entail a thorough exploration of the aims of the syllabus, whether implied or explicit, and of the ways in which the learners can make those aims their own. Such a process is more likely to succeed if it begins by inviting the learners to make explicit what they expect from the learning process and what they can bring to it, than if it begins with a lecture on the benefits of autonomous learning.

This may sound straightforward enough, but it cannot be achieved without changing the role of the teacher in a way that in turn changes the power structure of the classroom. Teachers who were themselves taught in the expository mode and whose training was in the same tradition, are likely to find it difficult to make the transition from purveyor of information to counsellor and manager of learning resources. For one thing, the expository mode requires the teacher to talk for a large part of each lesson, and this encourages him to believe that when he is not talking he is not teaching. How can the learners possible be learning when they, and not the teacher, are talking?

Another difficulty with the expository mode of teaching is that the teacher not only sets the problems but usually solves them too. In other words, teaching by example plays a much more central role than learning by doing. Even teachers who encourage their pupils to learn by discovering for themselves often find it difficult not to intervene when they see learners, individually or in a group, grappling with a problem and moving only slowly towards a solution. But it is precisely the grappling - the grinding together of conflicting constructs - that leads to learning, and much learner effort will be wasted if the teacher intervenes too quickly.

Teachers' eagerness to intervene is also prompted by their worry that there is so much ground to cover. As I noted in Chapter 5, this worry usually focuses on the grammar of the target language. We may accept the implication of research findings that the explicit teaching of grammar has at best a somewhat subordinate role to play in language teaching; but when the exam is looming and more than a few members of the class still can't seem to get their endings right, it can be very comforting for the teacher to run through the rules again.

For a teacher to commit himself to learner autonomy requires a lot of nerve, not least because it requires him to abandon any lingering notion that he can somehow guarantee the success of his learners by his own effort. Instead, he must dare to trust the learners. The expository teacher carries the whole burden of learning on his own shoulders: one of the chief reasons for trying to develop learner autonomy is to get the learners to share that burden.

The learner

At what stage are learners ready for autonomy? Teachers who ask this question usually expect an answer that proposes a minimum degree of maturity learners should achieve before they are encouraged to start accepting responsibility for their own learning. However, the answer to the question is, as soon as possible. Most of the techniques likely to be adopted in any scheme designed to promote autonomous learning at the second and third levels of education have been in common use at primary level for many years. That they have often been outstandingly successful is hardly surprising, for the primary child's personal constructs are still in the early stages of formation; she is only just beginning her acquaintance with institutionalized learning. Moreover, in their application at primary level these techniques deliberately seek to imitate the modes of learning that have shaped the child's development to date: problem-solving in a context of social interaction.

By the beginning of second-level education - which is when most language learning begins in formal educational contexts - learners have considerable experience of institutionalized learning, and they may be strongly resistant to the idea of autonomy. As Salmon (1988, p.61) points out,

> The progression of education is, broadly, a progression away from person-centred learning towards learning that is knowledge-centred. The hierarchy of school subjects reserves the highest status for forms of knowledge that are essentially depersonalized.

In other words, popular educational wisdom concedes that early learning needs to take account of the individuality of the learner - what he already knows, the system of values he brings with him to the learning task -, but assumes that the further we progress up the academic ladder the less these personal factors count.

For many learners at second and third levels the most important thing is not that they should learn, but that they should get good qualifications (cp. the first quotation from Illich on p.9 above). By the time learners are nearing the end of second-level education it may be difficult to shake their belief that the teacher's job is straightforwardly to prepare them to do well in the exams. This can be a problem especially with more able pupils, who may feel comfortable in a state of more or less total dependence on the teacher provided their efforts are duly rewarded.

By the time they reach third-level education, some learners have formed such a rigid view of what learning entails that they find it very difficult to become autonomous. Little and Grant (1986) describe one such case in their report on a pilot scheme designed to develop autonomous learning of German among undergraduate students of Engineering Science. The student in question believed himself to be a good language learner, despite the fact that languages had not been among his stronger subjects at school. His principal learning strategy was to try to learn chunks of the course materials by heart. Not surprisingly, this produced in him a feeling of acute boredom. Looming large in his thoughts was the image of one of his past teachers, for ever offering negative evaluations of his efforts. This learner frequently became discouraged by his lack of progress and several times was on the verge of leaving the scheme. Frequent counselling enabled him, precariously, to complete the two-year learning programme. By contrast, the most successful learner participating in the scheme was clear from the beginning where he wanted his learning to take him. He already knew quite a lot of

German, but he had learned it "naturalistically" (autonomously) by going to Germany to work during his summer vacations. His reason for joining the scheme was that he wanted to continue by other means what he had already started on his own initiative; in particular he wanted to give a vocational perspective to his learning. He subsequently found employment in a German laboratory.

We should not, of course, be surprised if some learners are resistant to the idea of autonomy. After all, autonomy implies a readiness to subject our certainties to continuous challenge, and that can be very unsettling. As a rule of thumb, the older learners are when they first meet the idea of autonomy, the harder the teacher will have to work to persuade them that it makes sense. Again, beginning with activities that demonstrate the personal basis of learning is likely to be more successful than a lecture explaining why learners need to be autonomous.

The process of learning

The autonomous language classroom or learning scheme will seek to create the conditions in which learning proceeds by negotiation, interaction, and problem-solving, rather than by telling and showing. These processes will focus the teacher's and learners' attention sooner rather than later on the content of learning and the organization of classroom activities.

In Holec's definition of learner autonomy, the learner accepts responsibility for the content of his learning. In some cases this may mean that the learner actually finds his own learning materials; though as we noted in Chapter 5, even self-motivating adult learners are likely to need assistance in finding materials, either because they do not know exactly what will correspond to their needs, or else because they do not know where to look for what they want. In any case, it is possible for the learner to accept responsibility for the content of his learning without necessarily choosing it himself. In Chapter 5 I referred to the experiment in which Jean-Pol Martin divided a French class into groups and the groups took turns to teach the rest of the class. In that instance, the language course book was chosen by the teacher, but the pupils accepted responsibility for the choice by agreeing to use it as the basis for their learning. And of course the group of learners responsible for teaching a particular unit to the rest of the class could not help but make it their own in the way they prepared and communicated it.

In most schemes designed to develop autonomous learning there is likely to be a compromise between learner-selected and teacher-selected materials, arising from the need to take account of the learners and their personal constructs on the one hand and the teacher's special expertise on the other. Where the selection of textbooks of any kind is concerned, the teacher has a responsibility that cannot be handed over to the learners because they do not have enough knowledge and experience to accept it. On the other hand, only learners can know what materials - from whatever source - are genuinely relevant to them. Thus it is essential that the content of learning should be subject to negotiation and continuous review. If it is not, learner responsibility is likely to be a rhetorical convention rather than a reality.

In Chapter 4 I argued that what we know about "naturalistic" second language acquisition encourages the view that learners in formal contexts need to be given access to as wide a range of discourse roles as possible: examples of how native speakers cope with different roles, together with opportunities to play the roles for themselves within the limits imposed by their competence in the target language. Thus it is a matter of the greatest importance how learning activities are organized. To some extent this will be determined by the choice of input materials. For example, the decision to use a course book but have the learners teach one another means that learners-as-teachers will inevitably be required to assume directive and expository roles; while learners-as-learners will assume responding roles and, depending on the nature of the course book, may also be assigned a variety of discourse roles in simulations of various kinds. At the other extreme, when it is decided that the learners should determine the content of learning by formulating group projects (as in the second classroom I described in Chapter 4, pp.30ff. above), the discourse roles that learners experience are not predetermined but depend on the ebb and flow of their interaction. This has the advantage of allowing discourse roles to be determined by the social dynamics of the group, but the disadvantage that learners may be trapped in the range of roles permitted them by the position they occupy in the social hierarchy of the class.

Learning resources and learning aids in the widest sense of the word - books, audio and video cassettes, computers - must be considered in terms of both the content of learning and classroom organization. Certainly learners need access to information about the target language. Specifically, they need dictionaries that will give them the words they want and grammars that will tell them how those words behave; dictionaries and grammars, moreover, that are easy for them to use. How audio and video materials are used will depend partly on how the content of learning is organized generally and partly on what facilities are available. In a class that is using one of the *Authentik* newspapers as a resource for project work, the facility of being able to view television news broadcast by satellite may provide a useful additional source of input. Similarly, a language laboratory that is organized partly as a self-access resource can support autonomous learning by making a host of supplementary materials available to the learners. It should be stressed, however, that an autonomous learning scheme does not depend above all else on providing a great wealth of materials. It is true that learners need much more input than they have customarily received, but it should be remembered that a single issue of one of the *Authentik* newspapers contains more input than many course books.

As Higgins (1988) has pointed out, computers can be used to support language learning in two different modes, which he labels "magister" and "pedagogue". In the "magister" mode the computer stands in for the expository teacher, giving the learner information, asking questions and providing the correct answer, sometimes with a certain amount of feedback on the learner's errors. In the "pedagogue" mode, on the other hand, the computer offers the learner various kinds of resource that he can draw upon as his needs develop. Both modes may have their place in an autonomous learning environment - "magisterial" programmes may be useful, for example, for learners who want to test their explicit knowledge of a particular grammatical feature. But on the whole the "pedagogue" mode is more likely to play a central role. Programs exist that enable learners to build up their own database, and this may be a useful way of getting a whole class to keep track of the vocabulary they learn. But perhaps the most beneficial use of the computer will be for word-processing. The possibility of being able to revise and correct *ad infinitum* encourages learners to experiment; the possibility of getting a "clean" print-out at any stage in the development of a written text is a powerful motivating factor.

Learner training

All "naturalistic" learning takes place in order to satisfy some need of the learner, and proceeds according to his own internal agenda. This applies equally to so-called developmental learning and learning that just seems to happen at later stages in life. Such learning, as I have argued at different points in this book, is autonomous; yet the learner is probably not aware of his autonomy and is unlikely to reflect much on the progress of his learning. Within formal educational contexts, on the other hand, it is fundamental to autonomous learning that the learner should develop a capacity to reflect critically on the learning process, evaluate his progress, and if necessary make adjustments to his learning strategies. For when we take a conscious decision to embark on a course of learning, we can only claim to be autonomous learners if we are able to exercise some degree of conscious control over the process. Learning how to learn is thus a central component of all autonomous learning schemes.

Many schemes require learners to keep a diary or journal in which they record what they have done, how well they think they have done it, and what they think they have learned. This serves the necessary purpose of giving retrospective shape to the learning process, making it tangible, something that can be recalled and talked about. However, teachers who have used diaries of this kind usually find that learners' judgements of their learning remain at a very general level, recording how hard they think they worked or how much they enjoyed a particular activity. This is hardly surprising, for without expert guidance few learners will be able to identify a specific learning strategy, let alone evaluate its effectiveness. Yet it is clear that to be able to do so belongs to a capacity for critical reflection on the learning process. Because it is not something that comes naturally, it requires a lot of effort and what (rather against the spirit of autonomous learning schemes) has come to be called "learner training".

Learning in formal educational contexts is a matter of conscious decision and conscious effort; at the same time, successful second language learning depends at least as much on the activation of largely unconscious acquisition processes as it does on deliberate effort. It is thus useful to distinguish between two different kinds of learning strategy, the behavioural and the analytical. Behavioural strategies are kinds of linguistic or communicative behaviour likely to promote unconscious learning as the target language is used, whereas analytic strategies are techniques for organizing and remembering things one is conscious of wanting to learn.

Behavioural strategies tend to resolve themselves into a single rule of thumb: never miss an opportunity to use (listen to, speak, read, and write) the language you are learning. In autonomous learning schemes that give learners access to a wide range of discourse roles, this may seem superfluous advice. But not every learner will necessarily accept all the discourse roles offered to him. Some roles may seem to run counter to his personality, while others may lie outside his experience to date. Helping a learner to accept such roles requires a great deal of tact; but it is a task that must not be shirked, for the growth of the individual's communicative capacity should be a feature not just of autonomous learning schemes but of education generally. As a matter of principle, learners should be encouraged to observe themselves as they use the target language, noting the circumstances in which they succeed and those in which they have difficulties, and exploring why the difficulties arise.

Analytical strategies are focussed on items of the target language that learners particularly want to remember - mostly words and phrases - and the rules that govern how those items behave. It is worth stressing again that learning rules is not likely to improve fluency in the target language, though it may well improve accuracy in situations where there is time to plan and/or revise. Again as a matter of principle, the better organized an analytical strategy is, the more successful it will tend to be. It is a good idea for learners to keep a vocabulary notebook in which they write down words they particularly want to remember. But it is not likely to help them much if they write words down in random or alphabetical order. Rather, they should be encouraged to organize the vocabulary they want to remember in semantic fields or thematic clusters, perhaps using different colours to distinguish between different word classes and arrows to indicate relations between words.

No two native speakers of a language have exactly the same vocabulary (any more than they have exactly the same personal constructs; the two facts are closely related). Thus in second and foreign languages too there will inevitably be individual variation. In autonomous learning schemes this should be seen as a positive rather than a negative factor. Learners should be encouraged regularly to explore the development of their target language vocabulary, asking themselves why they find it easy to remember some words whereas others never seem to be available when they need them. Since it is meant to be an aid to learning, the vocabulary notebook should reflect the fact that vocabulary acquisition is a dynamic process. There is clearly sense in not writing down something we already know; there might equally be sense in going through the vocabulary notebook at regular intervals and crossing out words that no longer require a conscious effort of recall.

Learning grammatical rules is usually thought of as something quite separate from vocabulary learning; though in fact when we remember a word, part of what we remember usually has to do with how it behaves in relation to other words. For this reason it is probably wise not to encourage a hard-and-fast division between vocabulary and grammar learning. Again, learners should be encouraged to commit grammatical rules to memory not because they are there, but because they are relevant to their particular communicative needs. Learning grammar should be based on exploration of language in use. For example, when they have completed a piece of written work, it can be useful for learners to consider the errors they have made and ask themselves why they made them. Getting learners to correct and edit one another's work can also be highly beneficial: another person's mistakes always seem to be easier to detect than one's own.

In vocabulary and grammar learning, learners should be encouraged always to make use of all the knowledge at their disposal, including knowledge of other languages, especially their mother tongue. Comparing patterns of regularity in the target language with patterns of regularity in the mother tongue can be one of the most effective routes to understanding. Moreover, learners should be encouraged to explore the usefulness of these analytic learning strategies as aids to communication. For example, if their work on vocabulary has taught them to note where cognates occur between the target language and their mother tongue, or to deduce the rules of word-formation in the target language, they are likely to be able to draw on that knowledge in certain communicative situations.

Finally, learners may need help in deciding how best to go about their learning - for example, when to learn something by heart, and when simply to write it down in an organized way and regularly review it. Sometimes they may seek advice on how best to proceed, but often they will approach a learning task assuming that they know how it should be tackled. In the latter case, are they expressing a learning preference that somehow reflects their cognitive constitution, or are they acting out the cultural conditioning they have received? This is a complex issue, and one that cannot be dealt with adequately here. However, since the processes that drive developmental learning and first language acquisition seem to be universal, it seems reasonable to assume that differences of experience (cultural differences in the widest possible sense of the term) account for very many of the individual differences between learners. Thus there is nothing sacrosanct about a particular learning style, and if it is inefficient, the learner should be encouraged to recognize the fact and explore alternative possibilities. This applies with no less force to learners from societies with very different traditions from our own. Certainly, it is important to respect ethnic and cultural differences and to recognize how easily we can give offence by seeming to dismiss lightly some highly valued feature of another way of life. At the same time, we must remember that all instructional methodologies are so many attempts to model internal psychological processes. As such they are cultural constructs, and like all other cultural constructs, they are constantly open to exploration, challenge and change.

Conclusion

"Exploration, challenge and change" sums up much of what this book has been about and is as good a note as any on which to end. In the compass of these sixty or so pages, I have tried to show why it makes sense to promote learner autonomy, from the perspectives of learning in general and language learning in particular; and I have tried to identify the principal practical issues involved in implementing learner autonomy and some of the problems likely to be encountered on the way. I do not believe that learner autonomy offers infallible solutions to every problem encountered in classroom learning; nor do I believe that it guarantees success in every case. But I do believe that it makes sense, not only as the logical outcome of learner-centredness in education generally, but also as the approach to language learning that can best do justice to communicative ideals and the insights we are beginning to gain from empirical research into language acquisition. Obviously, a book of this length can only seek to state principles, raise issues and offer general guidelines. But if in doing that it causes its readers - at any level of education - to reflect seriously on learner autonomy, it will have succeeded in its aim.

Suggestions for further reading

Two books by Jerome Bruner provide an eminently read-able introduction to his thinking on education: *The Process of Education* (Cambridge, Mass.: Harvard University Press; second edition 1977) and *Toward a Theory of Instruction* (Cambridge, Mass.: Harvard University Press; 1966). M. Boden's *Piaget* (Glasgow: Fontana; 1979) provides a wide-ranging introduction to the work of the Swiss polymath, while D. Wood's *How Children Think and Learn* (Oxford: Blackwell; 1988) includes an up-to-date survey of compet-ing models of cognitive development.

Ivan Illich's *Deschooling Society* (Harmondsworth: Penguin; frequently reprinted) is consistently thought-provoking on issues central to the arguments of this book. H. Kirschenbaum & V. L. Henderson's collection *The Carl Rogers Reader* (London: Constable; 1990) includes several of Rogers's essays on teaching and learning.

The essence of George Kelly's psychology of personal constructs is contained in his *A Theory of Personality* (New York: Norton; 1963), a reprint of the first three chapters of his earlier two-volume work, *The Psychology of Personal Constructs* (New York: Norton; 1955). The standard intro-duction to personal construct psychology is *Inquiring Man. The Psychology of Personal Constructs*, by D. Bannister & F. Fransella (London: Routledge; third edition, re-printed 1989). Phillida Salmon's constantly stimulating *Psychology for Teachers* (London: Hutchinson; 1988) looks at central issues in teaching and learning from the per-spective of personal construct psychology.

A. Elliot's *Child Language* (Cambridge Univerity Press; 1981) is a good introduction to first language acquisition, while *Language Development*, edited by A. Lock and E. Fisher (London: Croom Helm; 1984), offers an accessible overview of research findings. W. Littlewood's *Foreign and Second Language Learning* (Cambridge University Press; 1984) is an excellent brief introduction to second language acquisition.

Four books that grew out of a concern for the role of English in the British school curriculum contain a rich harvest of insights and practical ideas relevant to the promotion of learner autonomy in the foreign language classroom: *Language and Learning* by James Britton (Harmondsworth: Penguin; 1972); *From Communication to Curriculum* by Douglas Barnes (Harmondsworth: Penguin; 1976); *Language, the Learner and the School* by Douglas Barnes, James Britton and Mike Torbe (Harmondsworth: Penguin; third edition 1986); and *Finding a Language. Autonomy and Learning in School* by Peter Medway (London: Writers & Readers, in association with Chameleon; 1980).

Henri Holec's *Autonomy in Foreign Language Learning* (Oxford: Pergamon; 1981) retains its status as a foundation document in any discussion of autonomy in foreign language learning. The compendium of articles Holec edited for the Council of Europe, *Autonomy and Self-Directed Learning: Present Fields of Application* (Strasbourg: Council of Europe; 1988), reports on experiments in a number of different countries and educational settings. *Discourse and Learning*, a collection of papers produced by members of the Centre de Recherches et d'Applications Pédagogiques en Langues, Université de Nancy II, and edited by Philip Riley (London: Longman; 1985) has much to say about autonomy in language learning. *Self-Access Systems for Language Learning*, edited by David Little (Dublin: Authentik, in association with CILT; 1989), contains practical suggestions that are relevant to classroom as well as self-instructional learners. The papers collected in *Learning Styles*, edited by R. Duda and P. Riley (Presses Universitaires de Nancy; 1990), approach the question of learning styles from many different points of view and consider evidence drawn from a wide variety of learning environments.

Learner Strategies and Language Learning, edited by A. Wenden and J. Rubin (Prentice Hall International; 1987), reflects the recent growth of research into how learners go about the business of mastering a foreign language. *Learning to Learn English: a Course in Learner Training,* by. G. Ellis and B. Sinclair (Cambridge University Press; 1989), and *Language Learning Strategies,* by Rebecca L. Oxford (New York: Newbury House; 1990) offer a wealth of practical advice on how to help learners towards more efficient learning.

Communication in the Modern Languages Classroom, by Joe Sheils (Strasbourg: Council of Europe; 1988), is an indispensable compendium of pedagogical techniques designed to promote communicative language learning and thus of central relevance to learner autonomy.

Learner autonomy is also an underlying concern of *Authentic Texts in Foreign Language Teaching* (Dublin: Authentik; 1988) and a revised version of the same book, *Learning Foreign Languages from Authentic Texts* (Dublin: Authentik, in association with CILT; 1989), by David Little, Seán Devitt and David Singleton. Both books provide a theoretical discussion and many practical examples of the use of authentic texts in the foreign language classroom.

John Higgins's *Language, Learners and Computers* (Harlow: Longman; 1988) considers possible roles for computers in language learning in terms that are easily accommodated to discussion of learner autonomy. *CALL,* by David Hardisty and Scott Windeatt (Oxford University Press; 1989) is a useful guide to communicative language learning activities based on a variety of computer programs.

References

Bannister, D., & F. Fransella, 1989: *Inquiring Man. The Psychology of Personal Constructs.* London: Routledge. (Third edition, reprinted; first edition 1971.)

Barnes, D., 1976: *From Communication to Curriculum.* Harmondsworth: Penguin.

Bruner, J. S., 1966: *Toward a Theory of Instruction.* Cambridge, Mass.: Harvard University Press.

————————, 1977: *The Process of Education.* Second edition. Cambridge, Mass.: Harvard University Press.

Devitt, S. M., 1989: "Classroom discourse: its nature and its potential for language learning". CLCS Occasional Paper No.21. Dublin: Trinity College, Centre for Language and Communication Studies.

Frith, U., 1989: *Autism.* Oxford: Blackwell.

Higgins, J., 1988: *Language, Learners and Computers.* Harlow: Longman.

Holec, H., 1981: *Autonomy in Foreign Language Learning.* Oxford: Pergamon. (Reprint; first published 1979, Strasbourg: Council of Europe.)

Illich, I., 1979: *Deschooling Society.* Harmondsworth: Penguin. (Reprint; first published 1971, New York: Harper & Row.)

Janne, H., 1977: *Organization, Content and Methods of Adult Education.* Report CCC/EES (77) 3. Strasbourg: Council of Europe.

Kelly, G., 1963: *A Theory of Personality.* New York: Norton.

Kirschenbaum, H., & V. L. Henderson, 1990: *The Carl Rogers Reader.* London: Constable.

Little, D. (ed.), 1989: *Self-Access Systems for Language Learning.* Dublin: Authentik, in association with CILT, London.

Little, D., S. Devitt & D. Singleton, 1988: *Authentic Texts in Foreign Language Teaching: Theory and Practice.* Dublin: Authentik.

Little, D., S. Devitt & D. Singleton, 1989: *Learning Foreign Languages from Authentic Texts: Theory and Practice*. Dublin: Authentik, in association with CILT, London.

Little, D. G., & A. J. Grant, 1986: "Learning German without a teacher. Report on a self-instructional programme for undergraduate students of Engineering Science at Trinity College, Dublin, 1982-84". CLCS Occasional Paper No.14. Dublin: Trinity College, Centre for Language and Communication Studies.

Long, M. H., 1987: "Instructed interlanguage development". In L. M. Beebe (ed.), *Issues in Second Language Acquisition*, pp.115-41. New York: Newbury House.

Riley, P. (ed.), 1985: *Discourse and Learning*. London: Longman.

Salmon, P., 1988: *Psychology for Teachers. An Alternative Approach*. London: Hutchinson.

Sinclar, J. McH., & M. Coulthard, 1975: *Towards an Analysis of Discourse*. Oxford University Press.

Thomas, L., & S. Harri-Augstein, 1990: "On constructing a learning conversation". In R. Duda & P. Riley (eds.), *Learning Styles*, pp.207-21. Presses Universitaires de Nancy.